Scrub up, stand out & explode your professional brand.

LinkedIn Masterclasses

by Dionne Lew

Publication date: August 2016

Published by: Dionne Lew

First edition © Dionne Lew 2016

Paperback, Medium - Print, Paperback

Scrub up, stand out and explode your professional brand LinkedIn Masterclasses / by Dionne Lew

1. Business. 2. Internet. I. Title.

II. Title: Scrub up, stand out and explode your professional brand LinkedIn Masterclasses

ISBN 879-0-9953724-9-8

Cover and Book Design: Merryn Padgett, Earth & Sea Creative

Images: Courtesy of Pixabay and Death to the Stock Photo

CONTENTS

INTRODUCTION

Professionals know –

1. Social media is vital
2. They need to do something about it.

The problem? They're not sure what to do or where to start.

Scrub up, stand out and explode your professional brand helps close the knowledge gap and get you on the way.

How to use this book –

1. Section One - provides the theory behind the practice

2. Section Two - offers four easy-to-action Masterclasses that take you from wobbly beginner to confident Social Executive.

Let's go.

SECTION ONE: MYTH-BUSTING

First, let's get rid of the myths. This is the theory part.

A common sentiment I hear when speaking with professionals about the importance of social media for business is "Well, I'm successful and so are my peers and we don't use it". There are a couple of problems here.

While this can be true (and often is), a personal anecdote drawn from experiences under very different circumstances can't be extrapolated to understanding current trends. More importantly, it fails to take into account that there are billions of new consumers coming onto the market who have never lived without social media.

Social media is 14 years old if you count established platforms like LinkedIn, which has 433 million users, but online forums and networks predate this by many years. These people (consumers, voters) expect to find you in social not because you're cutting edge, but just as we presume we'll find inventory on shelves.

When Boston Consulting Group (BCG) put out its report on the internet economy in 2013, it showed that engaged, online businesses were outperforming peers by around 20 percent, a figure confirmed by Capgemini-MIT Sloane and McKinsey in 2014.

These figures are strong enough on their own but reveal only part of the story since only businesses that were still around could be surveyed. This is called 'survivor bias', and it means the impact may be greater since many businesses folded as online emerged.

With two billion people already using social media, you've got to take it seriously. With a flood of 'digital natives' into the market and digital growing at double-digit rates, it will be mission-critical in years ahead. Stewarding an organisation into the future is a leader's role.

Of course most leaders care greatly about company culture and results and implement numerous strategies to drive success and engagement. Social media is not a panacea nor does it claim to be. But it's a missing piece of the puzzle that many are seeking to understand and leverage.

Social shapes trust

We like to do business with people we know and trust. This much is not new. What's new is the impact of virtual relationships on that phenomenon.

The Edelman Trust Barometer, with its hefty sample of 35,000, reports a decline in trust year on year, particularly in institutions. Pew looked at trust from a generational perspective and found Millennials scored lower on trust than any other age group. On the other hand, trust in peers and subject matter experts is high and growing.

This is how it plays out. If I'm coming to see you and ask what café you recommend nearby, I am likely to act on that no matter how much clever marketing I get from other cafés in the area. From my perspective, I trust the advice because I know you gain nothing from giving me a good steer, other than the warm glow we get when someone likes a suggestion.

These conversations go on all the time in real life and there are billions of them happening in social media every day. In August 2015, for the first time, Facebook reached a milestone in which a billion people were active on a single day.

The question is: does this virtual trust matter? The answer is yes. We trust a virtual recommendation as much as one we get face-to-face. Around 70 percent of consumers trust online reviews. Bazaarvoice and Kelton Research show Millennials trust the expertise of strangers more than that of family and friends.

For example, if you're booking a room on Airbnb, you read the reviews. This is called user-generated content (UGC). These are strangers that you don't know and are unlikely to meet, yet their experiences have the biggest bearing on where you decide to spend money. This trend doesn't just apply to buying holidays and shoes. We're seeing it play out in investment choices through business and into politics.

Social influences investors

Investors are influenced by research they find on social media. According to Cogent Research, 90 percent of high net worth investor groups use social media. The report showed a third of affluent investors use social media specifically for personal finance and investing purposes. Importantly, as many as 70 percent changed relationships or reallocated investments as a result of content they'd found in the networks.

In the financial services sector, Cogent found that 46 percent of investors who used social media didn't have a financial advisor, and 52 percent said they would connect with an advisor through social media.

From a brand perspective, a further 28 percent of investors said they would see a financial company as "innovative" or a "leader in the industry" for offering social options.

In the US, most Fortune 100 companies use social media and in the UK the FTSE100 Social Media Index shows 86 percent of FTSE100 businesses used LinkedIn as part of communications strategy. Yet research by Web Profits last year on the social media activity of Australia's top publicly listed companies found almost half the top 100 companies don't bother. Use, however, is growing.

A study conducted in 2013 by Beaton Research and Consulting for Zurich on use of social media for financial advisors showed a "123 percent growth in advisers' usage of Twitter since December 2011 and a 74 percent growth in the use of LinkedIn" (arguably off a low base). According to a joint Putnam-FIT Consulting Survey of Financial Advisors' Use of Social Media, nearly half of advisors using social media for business acquired new clients through social networking.

Social is part of a multi-trillion-dollar economy

It's hard sourcing figures on social media value separate from digital and ecommerce because social media is part of a broader ecosystem. The numbers, however, are big.

BCG predicted that by 2016, online would contribute $4.2 trillion to the GDP of G20 nations, making it the equivalent of the fifth-biggest economy worldwide. More importantly from my perspective, BCG said it would contribute 5.5 percent to GDP.

In the UK, the internet is already the second-biggest economic contributor behind property, contributing 10 percent of GDP. In Deloitte's latest report, the digital economy in Australia has been valued at A$79 billion, 5.1 percent of GDP and bigger than agriculture, retail and transport.

The Australian economy has been bolstered by resources. A key question for Australia as the sector slows is how it remains competitive in a volatile global landscape. Online is a critical part of that mix.

Social impacts markets

In 2013, the Twitter account of Associated Press was hacked and a tweet was up for two minutes saying there'd been a bomb at the White House. The Dow Jones plummeted and $20 billion worth of stock changed hands during the brief trading hiccup. This raised questions both about the security of Twitter and the quality control of algorithmic traders.

In Australia the same year, Whitehaven Coal dropped six per cent after a fake press release that claimed to be from ANZ Bank, overturning a recent $1.2 billion loan to Whitehaven Coal. This would have had a significant impact on its Maules Creek project. Both Whitehaven and ANZ later confirmed the hoax, but not before $314 million was wiped off the share price and Whitehaven was placed in a trading halt.

The person who sent the fake release, anti-coal campaigner Jonathan Moylan, was subsequently investigated by the Australian Securities and Investments Commission (ASIC) for allegedly engaging in misleading and deceptive conduct.

Such events are creating shifts in the regulatory environment, probably slower than many industries would like. The lack of, or in some cases misdirected guidance on, social media by industry bodies has meant that many businesses have not had the confidence to strike out and leverage opportunities.

In April 2013, the US Securities and Exchange Commission (SEC) announced that social media could be used to let companies make corporate announcements. It's important to note that disclosure laws vary in Australia, which has an ASX-first approach (the ASX, a public company, operates Australia's main securities exchange). Working closely with ASIC, in 2013 the ASX updated its guidance on disclosure, advising companies to monitor online for sensitive information.

In September 2016, Bloomberg announced that customers would now be able to view a live feed of financial tweets into its terminals. It said the Twitter data would improve alerts and provide sentiment analysis and the ability to "graph historical Twitter volume related to securities or topics".

Social mentors help shape social leaders

Despite these dramatic impacts, there's a low level of awareness among senior leaders about social media. A McKinsey Global Survey in 2015 found 31 percent believe CEOs sponsor digital. Fewer still use it, despite mounting evidence that a social CEO positively impacts perceptions of trust, reputation and engagement.

We want social CEOs

1. Weber Shandwick – 81 percent of executives want a social CEO
2. Brandfog – two-thirds of customers trust companies with a social CEO more
3. Statista – 82 percent of employees think a social CEO positively shapes reputation.

Unfortunately, some leaders have been poorly advised on what social is, with a few signing up to having fake followers.

There are issues with executives and other leaders doing a hack job on social, coming across as broadcasting or sharing tweets clearly created by PR and not themselves. It's a problem that can be fixed.

Social is time-intense and there's nothing wrong with getting support. Co-management makes sense for a leader but they still have to show up in person. With three billion internet users and two billion on social and growing, a social CEO is a CEO for the times.

Social business, social professional, social leader

In an age of algorithms, who you are is in part determined by your digital footprint, which means that if you network for business, you will need to do so online. While business is in some ways the same as it ever was (based on mutually beneficial relationships), social media has turned the way we form those relationships on its head. No matter how well you're doing with your current communication, you need to look ahead and adapt the way you connect and communicate to keep up with this change.

Naturally, how you use the platform depends on what you want to achieve and that varies widely. Among other things you can use it to raise funds, for recruitment, for job search or networking with peers.

For leaders like you, a great place to start is LinkedIn. Like 433 million other professionals you've probably signed up. Now find out how to *Scrub up, stand out and explode your professional brand.*

SECTION ONE: WHY LINKEDIN?

LinkedIn is not the only social media channel that can help you grow influence and reach, but it's the one most professionals feel comfortable with.

LinkedIn is an economic and influence powerhouse

If you think LinkedIn is just a good "place to put your CV", you're missing out on the platform's huge business benefits and potential.

LinkedIn is a powerhouse of economic data that can predict and fill skills gaps, uncover rare, high-demand talent and it's now one biggest publishing houses in the world. With a 433 million-strong readership it can even, strangely enough, create a sales spike for traditional publishers.

Equity raisings have been done on LinkedIn. One Australian business expanded into 27 countries using a LinkedIn-only approach. BT used LinkedIn to drive five times more social interaction. NBC Congress Centre amplified the reach of its content by almost 50 percent.

Thought leaders, venture capitalists, talent-seekers, those who want to grow clout internally or transition careers, even students who need to know what degrees will get them a foot in the door with their dream company. Everybody can leverage this professional network.

Equity raising

Of course, in any regulated area following the rules in your jurisdiction is non-negotiable but LinkedIn allows you to:

1. Tell your story directly
2. Identify value-added potential investors, including past investors in comparable funds

3. Engage with experts, potential investors, entrepreneurs, investment banks and intermediaries' thought content, groups and mail at every stage of the investment cycle

4. Grow a trusted network through common connections, reaching out to relevant people and nurturing the connections you already have.

A quick search for equity raising on LinkedIn puts you directly in front of relevant experts, groups and content, whether you're looking to attract funding or seeking the right opportunity to invest.

David Teten, Chairman of the Harvard Business School Alumni Angels, says social media is key to investment strategy and that of the 1,000 venture capitalists in the US actively seeking deals, about 10 to 15 percent blog.

Social media can be used through the whole investment cycle to raise capital, originate investments, for due diligence and exit investment.

We know investors act on the information they find on LinkedIn. According to Cogent Research, high-wealth investor groups use social media to inform investment decisions and up to 70 percent have changed relationships or reallocated investments as a result.

You can get your content out through status updates, as posts or using the slide-sharing platform SlideShare, which allows you to include rich media like video that can be viewed anywhere, anytime and also showcased on your profile.

These actions will help you find investment on LinkedIn

Map the kinds of people you need to reach at each stage of the investment cycle

Use advanced LinkedIn search to identify them, reach out through common connections or directly

3. Develop a content strategy that gets your narrative in front of them including through SlideShare

4. Interact directly, in comments, through groups and by sharing – create a community and generate interest.

Business growth

CEO Craig McDonald expanded his company MailGuard into 27 countries with a LinkedIn-only approach heavily based around publishing content.

McDonald says one reason LinkedIn content is so powerful is that people tend to read content after-hours when they're more open and accessible to the message. MailGuard also has a great blog that shares useful content.

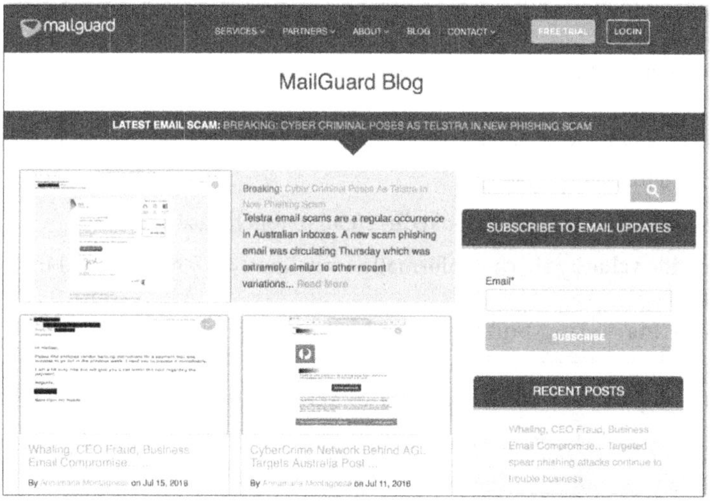

When someone clicks on your profile and sees you're publishing or sharing, there's immediate resonance and a reason to engage. It pretty much takes cold calling out of the equation.

Timothy Hughes, the No. 1 social selling expert in the world, says social media has fundamentally impacted the sales process and will continue to transform the way we grow business into the future, with 25 percent of business-to-business salespeople jobs no longer existing.

Hughes says the biggest change has been in the buying process because people use Google to search and make purchasing decisions without necessarily involving a salesperson.

Hughes says 72 percent of buyers are going through such a process and only when they get 50 to 80 percent of the way through the buying cycle do they actually engage with the salesperson.

Tim's bestselling book *Social Selling* looks in detail at how salespeople can use social media including LinkedIn to boost sales.

These actions will help sell on LinkedIn

1. When you make a contact, immediately extend the invitation on LinkedIn
2. Send a follow-up message
3. Set a reminder notice in LinkedIn email to touch base
4. Provide value by sharing information you know they're interested in.

Cut your marketing budget and add it back in where it counts

Want to cut your marketing budget by 25 percent? Think about using LinkedIn to ask industry experts, employees or prospects what they think about an issue, your product, a new initiative. The list is endless.

You can tap into the collective intelligence of industry-specific groups and use status updates to ask questions or share polls. Redirect the money you save as an investment into building a strong, strategic and committed social media team that will amplify your brand and generate leads.

Take these marketing actions on LinkedIn

1. Create a LinkedIn poll to get answers to questions and amplify the results by sharing them on other social media channels
2. Post a status update that asks a question or engages your followers around an interesting topic
3. Ask groups for input about gaps in the market, product names, customer experience, dos and don'ts. People are generous and willing to share experiences online.

Rare talent, real-time skill

LinkedIn data shows we currently can't fill the demand for jobs like software engineering because companies can't afford to wait two to four years to find talent. Immersive six- to 12-week boot camps have emerged as a way to fill that gap.

One in 100 LinkedIn members did boot camps in 2011. By 2014 that number had grown to 8,000 and this year it's predicted there will be 16,000 boot camp graduates.

Who should care about this? Employers wanting talent. Human resource professionals looking to grow internal talent. Governments needing to partner with private industry to generate future jobs. Entrepreneurs looking for business opportunities.

While LinkedIn data can validate a training approach like boot camps, it's about something much deeper: the ability to predict skills and close gaps using real-time economic data that maps employers' needs with skill availability and then provides training solutions on platforms like Lynda.com, which LinkedIn recently acquired.

There can be unintended benefits to this non-traditional training approach. For example, women are under-represented in technology but comprise 40 percent of boot camp graduates. Sixty-five percent of HackerYou's graduates are women, compared with 27 who come out of the 150-plus university programs.

Do the boot camps work?

According to the LinkedIn official blog, top-10 companies employing boot camp graduates include Google, Apple, Facebook, Microsoft, IBM, JPMorgan Chase, Salesforce, Accenture, American Express and LinkedIn.

We also know that of the rising business stars referred to as 'new wavers', 80 percent didn't go to an Ivy League university for their undergraduate education and only 15 percent earned an MBA.

Training and recruitment actions to take on LinkedIn

1. Build a company page
2. Encourage employees to use LinkedIn to amplify your brand
3. Check out Lynda on LinkedIn.

Pick yourself, grow authority and influence

Nowadays you can reject the tyranny of being picked, as Seth Godin says. Instead you can pick yourself by creating excellent content and sharing it on social media channels to grow influence and authority.

This does not mean traditional media is dead, more that media as a whole has morphed. For example, some YouTube channels get more views a day than all the combined news programs in Australia. TV is still important as part of a mix, as are other channels, but they feed off each other.

We saw this recently with the leadership change in Australia, where #libspill trended on Twitter and drove people back to independent bloggers and also traditional media channels, then back to social channels for discussion and further links. There's no either/or in this space anymore.

LinkedIn is a significant publishing house, one of the biggest in the world, with one million unique publishers producing more than 130,000 posts a week.

That's an opportunity to showcase thought leadership and get content in front of decision-makers rather than tangled up in the middle management tree. Over 45 percent of readers are in the upper ranks of their industries – CEOs, presidents, vice presidents and so forth – the kind of people who might be interested in your investment opportunity or growth strategy.

According to LinkedIn, major book publishers like Simon & Schuster report spikes in sales every time their business authors write on the networking platform. The LinkedIn writers, in turn, are being approached by the media for comment once they're recognised as experts in a particular field.

When you publish on LinkedIn, your material shows on your profile, a form of 'social proof' that you're real and you know what you're talking about. It's also a calling card to connect with other content producers and so expand your networks.

Actions to help you be a thought-leader on LinkedIn

1. Get clear on your strategic intent and develop a content strategy to deliver it
2. If you don't have time to write original content, read and post comments on others' content
3. Use free professional curation sites like Meddle, which allow you to extract content from an original article, make a comment and then distribute the 'mini-blog' widely. This way, many small impressions over time contribute towards create a digital footprint.

LinkedIn is, of course, also an excellent source of CVs and 94 percent of recruiters use it to identify and approach talent. The new LinkedIn jobs app means you can search by role and location and use your profile to apply with a click.

So what would you send to an employer if you were suddenly asked to submit an application for a dream role?

That's what your LinkedIn profile should look like because increasingly that's what you will send. A clear headshot, narrative written in the first person, a 'searchable' bio that helps you stand out from the crowd.

Now let's go do that.

SECTION TWO: MASTERCLASS ONE: HOW TO SCRUB UP & STAND OUT

Signing up to LinkedIn without doing anything is like going to a networking event and standing in the corner. To make it work, you've got to do something once you're there.

LinkedIn is a powerhouse of data, connections and content that you can use to position yourself and your business, all of which starts with a smart, optimised profile.

This Masterclass series provides a number of quick and easy-to-implement actions that take you from the fundamentals through to advanced tips and tricks that will make you a LinkedIn star. Let's start with the basics.

Put your best profile forward

Just as people are anchored by what they see when you walk through the door, digital imprints are the contemporary first impression.

These impressions count. We use anchors and reference points to evaluate and make decisions and they influence us even when we're presented with information to the contrary, which is why it's hard to turn things around if you get off on the wrong foot.

While ultimately we rise and fall by the quality of our work, when it comes to building contacts or growing leads, social proof is a way to get your foot in the door.

Here's how to build a LinkedIn profile that sends the right message.

This is not a brand

Your LinkedIn profile is an important plank of your professional brand so how it looks and reads is important.

Our brains are wired to respond quicker to visuals than words. Think through the mark you want to leave and use images and colours to achieve it.

A hard-hitting lawyer has a different tone from a mindful one, an executive coach from a lifestyle coach with a focus on fun. Use photographs, images, colours and words that reflect your promise.

Are you a forensic auditor with an eye for detail? A pink balloon may not send the right message. Likewise, a yoga instructor targeting time-poor executives may not want a burnished, loud and proud look.

Tips

1. Ensure the look and feel of your LinkedIn profile embodies your brand promise
2. Ensure your LinkedIn profile is consistent with other digital and social media assets like a website or Twitter profile
3. Upload a professionally designed banner that showcases your business offering or expertise
4. Use a professional logo
5. Write and rewrite your profile so that it's brief but informative
6. Avoid jargon and 'corporatese'
7. Avoid writing in capital letters
8. Check grammar and spelling.

This is not a headshot

Unless you're a model or an agency or this look is totally on-brand, it's not an appropriate headshot. Nor is a smartphone photo with the dog or kids cut out. Invest in a professional headshot that's properly sized for social media platforms.

Gone are the days where including a photograph in your resume was a shortcut to the bin. In a world where so much contact and especially first contact is online, people like to see who's on the other side. Photographs are a link between the digital and real worlds.

The default avatars, or 'eggheads' as they're known, are instantly off-putting. The bots that trawl the web identifying spam target them as questionable.

It's important to use a current photo so that when you bring a contact into real life (IRL) there's continuity. You want to be able to walk into a room, instantly recognise who you're meeting and seamlessly pick up where the online thread left off.

Having said that, once you've got a professional image in place you can change it up a bit and have fun, for example at Christmas by popping on a Santa hat or a touch of glitter. In the main, though, keep it professional.

Tips

1. Have a professional photograph taken with a few different angles
2. Use the series across different profiles for a related look and feel without being same-same
3. Avoid using default avatars or eggheads. If you don't want the general public to see your photo, go to Settings (hiding behind your photograph on the top righthand side). Click on Privacy and Settings and under Basics select who can see your profile picture.

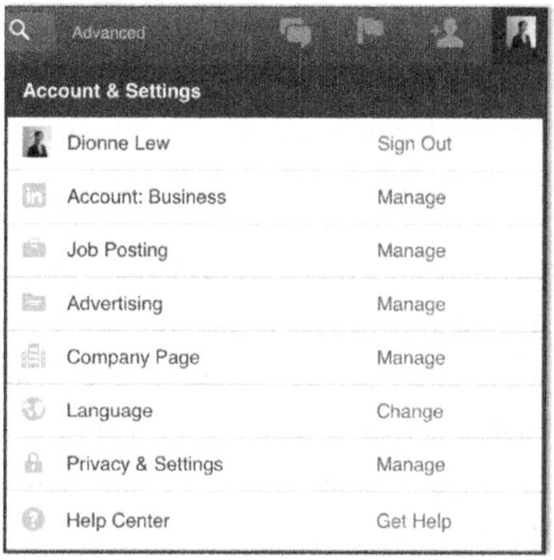

This is not a biography

So you're a CEO, marketer, nurse, lawyer? On a platform of 433 million global professionals, a title is not a differentiator.

The small amount of space that LinkedIn allows for your profile is prime real estate. Use it to differentiate yourself.

This part of the profile is also searchable so add key words that other people would use if they were looking for someone with your skills. When you're doing this, try thinking from their headspace.

For example, say someone wants a financial planner. No matter how great you are, they're unlikely to type in 'Jane Smith'. Instead, they'll use terms like 'financial planning', 'finance', 'Melbourne/London/Dubai', 'high growth'. Load it up with relevant terms and make sure you get a key skill in at least once.

I speak, write and consult on social media for executives and boards. Notice how I've filled my headline with meaningful, searchable terms that go to the heart of where I can help.

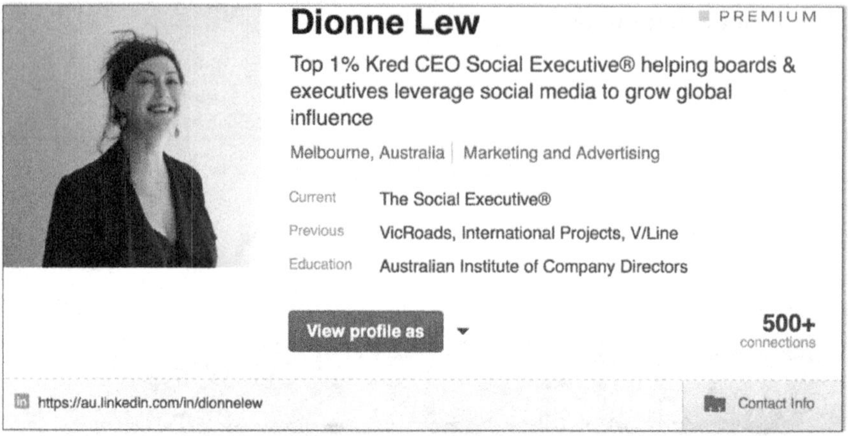

This is not your history

There's no need to write *War and Peace*. Even getting someone to scroll up a page requires effort and attention, which are rare commodities. Dot points with little information are also not helpful.

Instead, write a brief overview for the various positions you've held, focusing on what you've achieved rather than your responsibilities. What people are looking for is a logic around progression that talks to growing experience and also credibility.

When you set up a position, LinkedIn asks you to add in the company you worked for and automatically gives the option to load the logo, which is drawn from the company page. This is frequently used for authentication so do it properly. People can use search to confirm the company exists and find others who work there to verify your claim if required.

You can see here that I worked for VicRoads and that I have recommendations associated with it. This is more 'social proof' that I'm who I say I am and have done what I say I've done. More about recommendations later.

Director Corporate Communications

vicroads

VicRoads

October 2006 – October 2012 (6 years 1 month) | Melbourne, Australia

I was the Director of Corporate Communications, reporting to the CEO, member of the Executive Corporate Management Group, Chair Communications Governance Board and Member Personal Productivity Board.

I led the Marketing, Communications & Design, Media and Web & Online Engagement teams with matrix management responsibilities for a 70-strong team Statewide. With a strong track record of successful innovation in particular in the digital/social media area, VicRoads was cited by the Auditor General in 2012 for effective use of non-traditional media and carefully planned communications strategy and received over 42 awards in marketing/communications (predominantly in road safety).

- Member, Australian Institute of Company Directors (2012)
- Chair, Communications Governance Board (since 2010)
- Review Board Member, Victorian Health Department (2011)
- Member, Communications Executive Board
- Member, Communications for a Cause (pro bono)
- Member, Public Relations Institute of Australia

All achievements are a team effort and I was genuinely fortunate to work with many very talented individuals during my time at VicRoads.

▸ 1 organization

▾ 5 recommendations, including:

Gary Liddle
Chief Executive Officer, Public Transport Victoria

Dionne joined VicRoads in 2006, transforming corporate affairs into an innovative and integrated function that has been... View ↓

Judith Pettitt
Executive Director Corporate Services at VicRoads

Dionne was responsible for taking VicRoads on an amazing communications and social media journey that positioned us at the... View ↓

Because LinkedIn company pages require administrators, there's a level of verification built into the process. If someone claims to have worked at a place or gone to a university or school that doesn't have an official link, check it out. Unless there's a spelling error it could signal a false claim.

LinkedIn also allows you to add rich media to each position, a great opportunity to prove you do what you say you do. Just select the format you want to upload at the bottom of the section. It goes without saying that if it's confidential company IP, it doesn't get posted.

So you're an academic? Add a keynote presentation. A speaker? The show reel. A construction manager? A link to an award-winning portfolio. Again, it's about validating your claims.

In the next class you'll learn to finesse the basics by crafting a vanity URL and integrating LinkedIn with other social platforms and global messaging apps. You'll also find out how to manage endorsements and recommendations or turn them off.

MASTERCLASS TWO: AMPLIFY YOUR PRESENCE – THE WHY AND HOW

We just learned about the importance of creating a standout profile to showcase professional expertise within LinkedIn's 433 million-strong global community.

Let's step it up with a focus on creating a customised, consistent social presence and amplifying reach by adding in other channels.

We'll also learn how a LinkedIn profile helps keeps your digital nose clean and can push you up the Google ranks, pivotal for Online Reputation Management (ORM).

Claim your 'vanity URL'

First, let's make sure you have a consistent online name.

When you first set up a LinkedIn profile, you get a default address (also called an URL) that looks something like this - au.linkedin.com/in/janesmith76587. It shows what country you're in and a name followed by a random string of numbers.

You need to get rid of the messy numbers and create a URL that's as close as possible to your real name. On LinkedIn, this is called your 'vanity URL'.

Given that millions use LinkedIn, common names are not always available so try variations that include middle initials or putting your surname first. Whatever combination you settle on, it must be easily identifiable because you want your profile to be found.

It's easy to change – just edit your Profile.

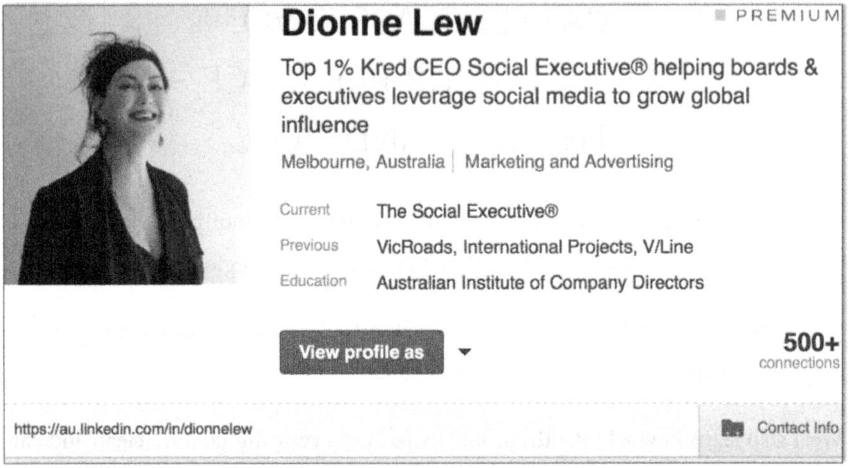

1. Move your cursor over Profile in the menu at the top of your LinkedIn page and select Edit Profile.

2. Under your profile photo on the lefthand side you'll see a URL. Mine is shown here as https://au.linkedin.com/in/dionnelew but yours is likely to have the default formatting. Look for the Settings icon next to it, which looks like a little grey wheel.

3. A pop-up message Update your public profile settings appears as you scroll over so click the wheel.

4. It will open to a page that says Your public profile URL on the righthand side, with a pen icon for editing.

5. Click the pen icon. You can then change the highlighted text in the box.

   Add your name without spaces, symbols or special characters (whether you use upper or lowercase doesn't matter).

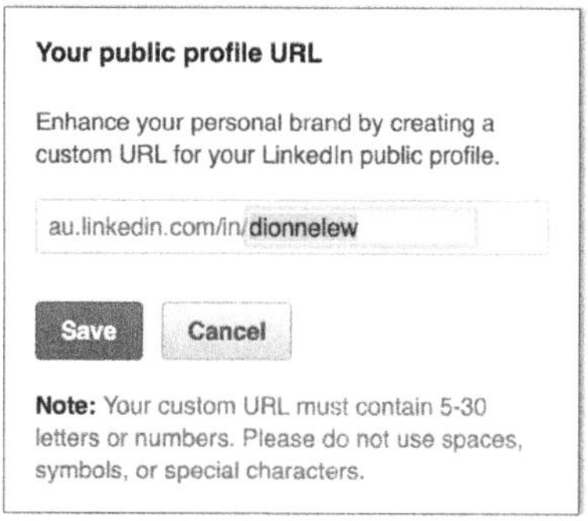

6. Remember to Save. Adding a LinkedIn URL to your email signature or on other collateral is a great way to direct people to your profile.

Why professionals need an online presence

It's been said that the best place to hide a dead body is page two of Google. That's because if you're not on page one of search results, you don't exist. Is it important to exist online? It's vital.

A digital footprint is part of who you are. When we want to find someone, we hit the web.

There are over a trillion searches on Google a year, not counting the other search engines and 56 percent of people Google themselves. Over time, if you're a not-for-profit leader in clean water and publish and comment on this, your name comes up in association with these terms. You want this. It validates expertise and gives others a way to find you. This can considerably increase your chances of being recruited into international positions or onto boards, a foot in the door after which your genuine experience can be authenticated.

There is, as ever, a dark side. We form views of people, products or services via reviews, referrals and other online data. If someone says negative things that are untrue or old but that comes up first, that's how you'll be viewed.

You can't erase your online history but you can manage it. That said, in 2014 the European court ruled that people had a 'right to be forgotten', and Europeans can demand that search engines remove links to accurate information. French regulators are now requiring search engines to censor results in the US, not just Europe, and some claim that this is a huge threat to an open internet.

Hot legal issues aside, individuals can manage ORM with digital and social assets that generate content and links they want to be known for and that drive them up the ranks.

But how do you get onto to page one?

Companies spend lots of money to build and optimise websites (called 'search engine optimisation') with keywords, valid links, PR and marketing, but individuals don't usually have these resources at their disposal.

This is where social media profiles come into their own. When you create a LinkedIn profile, a public version is included in the member directory and can be found by search engines.

Customise your public profile

It's up to you to decide what people who are not in your network see. On LinkedIn, you can show as much or little as you want to the general public.

You may be happy for me as a colleague to see a photo because LinkedIn will know who I am and that I'm looking at you, but not as happy for a curious member of the public to see what you look like.

To customise what people see, go through steps 1, 2 and 3 to your Public Profile Settings and scroll down to Customise your Public Profile.

1. Customise your Public Profile

2. You can make the profile visible to no one or everyone.

   There's little point having a hidden profile if you're using LinkedIn for professional branding, but you might want to take it offline to create it or if you want a break for personal reasons.

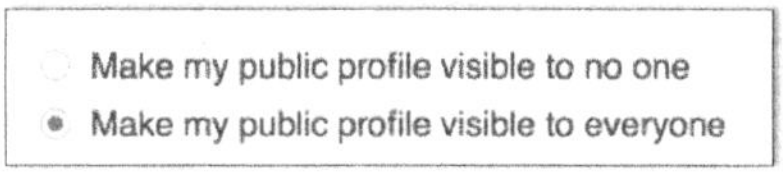

3. LinkedIn basics are included by default.

   Tick to include pictures, headlines, websites, posts etc as you prefer.

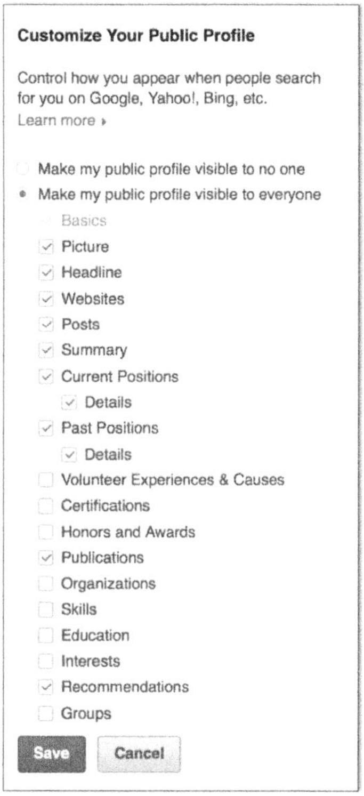

Amplify your presence by integrating Twitter and WeChat

Ramp it up by connecting social media channels like Twitter and WeChat messenger directly into LinkedIn. This extends your presence, creates consistency and saves time as you can automatically share what you do on LinkedIn outside the platform, reaching a far greater audience.

Establishing a social media ecosystem (a combination of social media channels like LinkedIn with Facebook and Twitter, or WeChat with Pinterest and Instagram depending on what works best personally for you and in your industry) takes work. However, once it's set up, it means that one action – a post, a comment, a share – can get huge reach with just a click.

Twitter is a microblog that allows you to share 140-character messages with links to photos or articles. It's the only truly open, global platform and I believe it's critical for extending professional reach beyond 'known' friend-of-friend style networks.

WeChat is a messaging app with apps for commerce, social and gaming built into it (10 million third-party apps in fact). It's huge in China and less understood in the West but very powerful, with 500 million users and growing. On WeChat I can lean over, scan the barcode on the biscuits that I just finished on my desk and because my digital wallet is built in, order biscuits that will be delivered to me the next day.

For those who do business around the globe, the integration allows networking across all channels, magnifying a professional or business presence.

1. To integrate Twitter and WeChat, go to your photo (I trust you changed the default avatar) on the righthand side of your page and hover. A menu will drop down that allows you to select Privacy and Settings.

2. Under Third Parties you'll see options for managing Twitter and WeChat.

3. Let's start with Twitter.

   LinkedIn will show any Twitter profiles already connected.

   Add others or delete a profile here and remember to tick the Account Visibility box.

4. Click the green plus sign. This will automatically open a screen asking you to authorise the app. Click Authorise App.

5. Now for WeChat. Under Third parties, click the WeChat settings.

6. A window opens with the green plus sign. Add WeChat with the QR code provided to you when you download the messenger app.

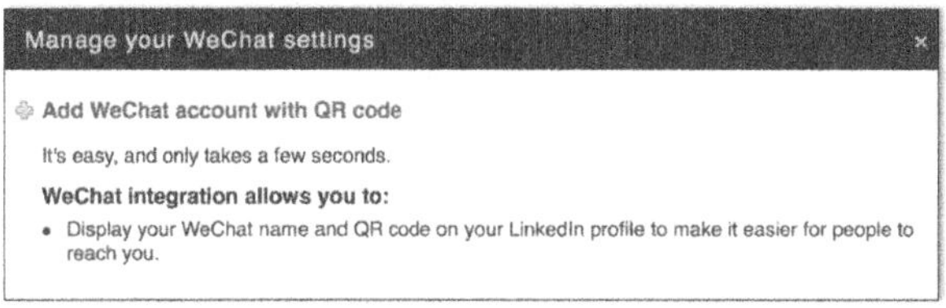

7. On your smartphone, scan the barcode using the WeChat app. LinkedIn will send your name and profile URL to WeChat and connect them.

A vanity URL and tailored public profile will enhance your professional image. Integrating Twitter and WeChat, if you have them, will amplify reach. Next we'll learn to enrich a profile with media, documents and what content marketing authority Trevor Young calls the 'quiet giant' of the social web, SlideShare.

We'll also explore how to keep your profile uncluttered and in line with industry regulations and legal obligations by properly managing recommendations and endorsements (those thumbs-ups you've received from people you've never seen in your life). Should you accept them? Probably not. I'll tell you why next.

MASTERCLASS THREE: ENRICH AND SIMPLIFY YOUR PROFILE, GET 10x MORE ATTENTION

So far, so good.

You've learned to create a standout LinkedIn profile and a customised, consistent social presence, amplified through global social media channels that are pivotal to ORM (that's online reputation management, remember).

Now you can ramp it up a notch by enriching and simplifying your profile, adding rich, visual media to showcase expertise while eliminating the dross.

Just because a LinkedIn profile is succinct doesn't mean it can't convey depth.

On the other hand, LinkedIn provides many ways to showcase expertise by adding documents, infographics, photos, videos and presentations like SlideShare.

Zuckerberg types aside, the apparent meteoric rise of someone from university to CEO with two lines about each of his/her two roles doesn't inspire confidence. People want to get under the skin of what you're really about.

Who are you? What do you do? What skills do you have that could be mutually beneficial? What case studies support your claims? A summary is not the place for detailed information, but if it catches someone's attention, give them somewhere to go.

Enriching a profile with real examples of work confers credibility and makes you relatable.

The enriched media you add should be visually focused because the brain is wired to respond to visual communication.

- We take in images 10 times faster than other kinds of information
- It takes 150 milliseconds to process an image and 100 milliseconds to attach meaning to it
- Colour increases recall of technical information by up to 82 percent.

A profile works better if you 'display, not say' because it:

- Gets more attention – content with images gets 94 percent more views
- Gets more shares - visual content is 40 times more likely to get shared, infographics are shared three times more than other types of content
- Is more helpful - people following directions with text and illustrations do 323 percent better than those who don't get illustrations.

Enrich your profile to illustrate expertise

1. Find Profile on the top menu bar and select Edit Profile from the dropdown menu.

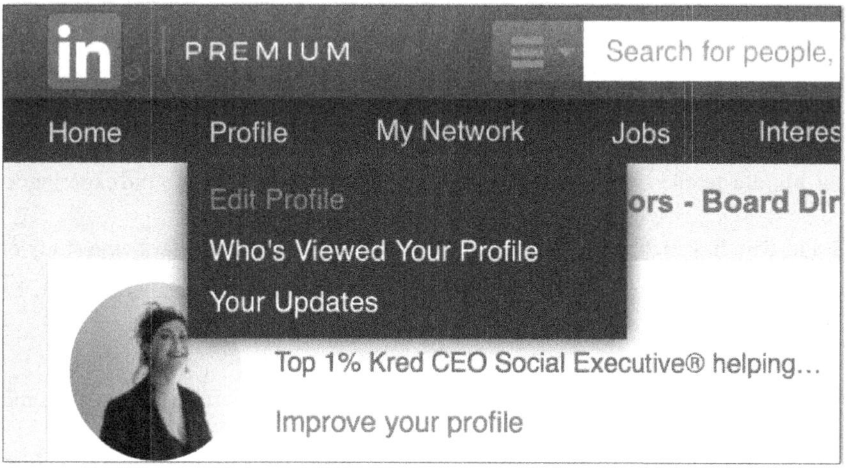

Your profile opens in editable mode.

2. Scroll to the media bar at the bottom of the section you want it displayed in and choose what you want to add (for example, Document). Click the Document icon and a new menu opens underneath.

3. LinkedIn uses a service called Embed.ly. If the content you want to add comes from a Supported Provider, add the link (for example, to a Flickr photo account). LinkedIn supports many providers. However, if the content you have isn't on the list, don't worry.

4. To add media, you can also click Upload File from the same section and save it. Viola!

Less is more, so choose content that goes to the heart of what you're about. For example, the manager of social at KLM, Karolin Vogel-Meijer, has added a 34-minute detailed video on the KLM social program to her background experience.

It's in Dutch, which makes sense for her audience, but it's a brilliant case study of using end-to-end social including to generate new revenue streams and can be found at Jay Baer and Karolin. The video is proof-positive of her claims.

Repeat for any section, but it must add to the narrative. Clutter is distracting and unprofessional. Keep your profile lean and clean while backing up claims.

Simplify

Un-endorsing endorsements

Some profile clutter on LinkedIn is bestowed on you rather than created by you.

Are you receiving endless endorsements from people you've never met and who have no idea what you do? You're not alone.

Not only are they frustrating, there may be legal consequences for displaying them. Jamie White from PodLegal says that "displaying a false endorsement or testimonial on your website, or anywhere for that matter, could amount to misleading and deceptive conduct".

Switching off endorsements isn't my preference. The recommendations of people we know and trust powerfully influence decisions, and appropriately so. Whether someone has a history of excellence or falling out with others, you want to know about it.

However, you may work in an industry where accepting endorsements is tricky.

For example, in the US, financial advisors are not allowed to use client testimonials in advertising under 206(4) of the Investment Advisers Act of 1940. Legally it's murky as to whether an endorsement is advertising, but it makes advisors nervous despite guidance by the Financial Industry Regulatory Authority.

In Australia, the Australian Prudential Regulation Authority, the ASX and the Australian Competition and Consumer Commission provide some guidance. Social impact on markets, including on investment decisions, is not well understood.

Before you go into an endorsement-removing panic, remember that regulators must maintain a balance between law and engagement. I don't envy them that difficult challenge, although they must be in step with the times.

Here's one example. In 2014, health professionals took on the regulator, the Australian Health Practioners Regulation Agency (APHRA), arguing that its guidelines were created by people with no understanding of how social works.

The regulator subsequently adjusted its guidance but barely showed up online (twitter Q+A #ahpraqanda). However constrained regulators like APHRA are by law, they should still participate in the debate.

Social media is an extraordinarily valuable 'listening' tool and can be viable in regulated industries provided the boundaries are crystal clear.

From my perspective, leaders, boards and regulators need proper education to ensure they're digitally and socially literate and that decisions on social media are properly informed. Some remain anchored by myths about social media that are outdated.

Having said all of that, if you prefer to switch off rather than manage endorsements, it's easy to do.

How to switch off endorsements

1. Find Profile and select Edit Profile from the dropdown menu. Scroll right down to the bottom of the editable page until you reach Skills & Endorsements.

2. Because you've opened your Profile in editable mode, when you hover on the righthand side of the Skills & Endorsements section you'll see an icon to add skills, or a two-headed arrow that allows you to reorder the endorsements you receive. Select Add skill.

3. In the settings you have the option to toggle between Yes and No for I want to be endorsed. Select No. Save.

Endorsements no more.

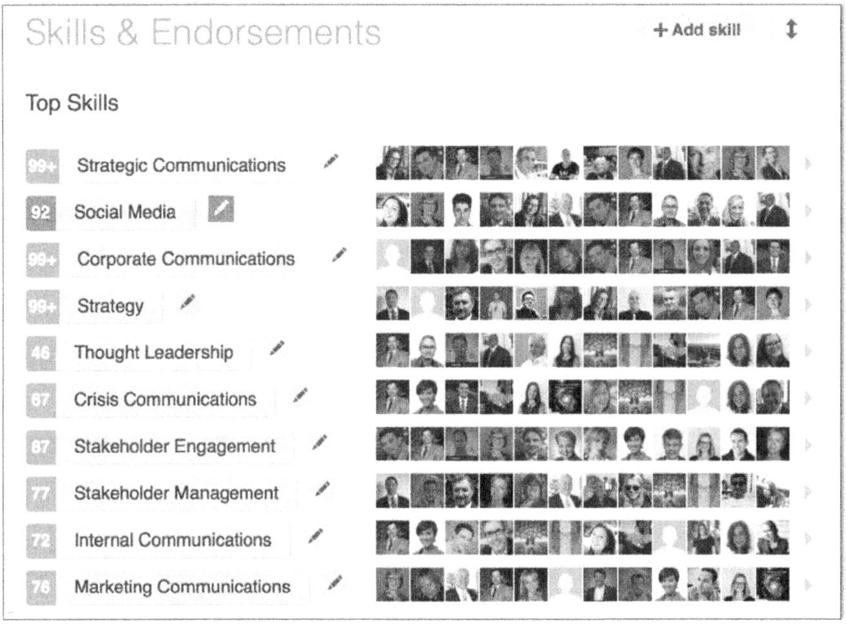

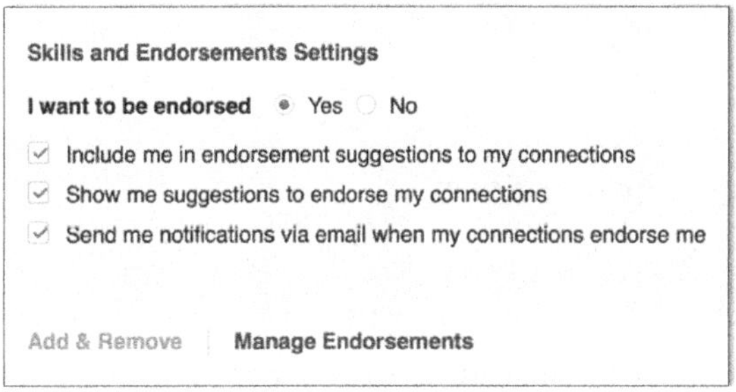

How to manage endorsements

Alternatively, and preferably for me, you can manage the skills for which you've received endorsements. Follow the previous steps to get to Skills & Endorsements.

1. At the bottom you'll see options to Add & Remove or Manage Endorsements. Choose Manage Endorsements. Open the skill you want to edit.

2. Clicking the uppermost box completely switches off endorsements for this skill. In the image below, the number count for Strategic Communications decreases as shown from 217 to 0.

   Don't worry – you haven't lost them. They're just in hiding. You may want to do this if you move into a regulated industry or one where the skill is not a priority. This is important for managing career transitions where you want to emphasise certain skills over others.

3. You can remove a single endorsement from someone you don't know or who doesn't know your work (I know all the above endorsees well, as they do me) by clicking on the box directly next to their name. Remove false endorsements one by one.

4. Remember to Save. Switch off Notify your network? so that your contacts aren't continually told you're making changes, in particular for a big cleanup.

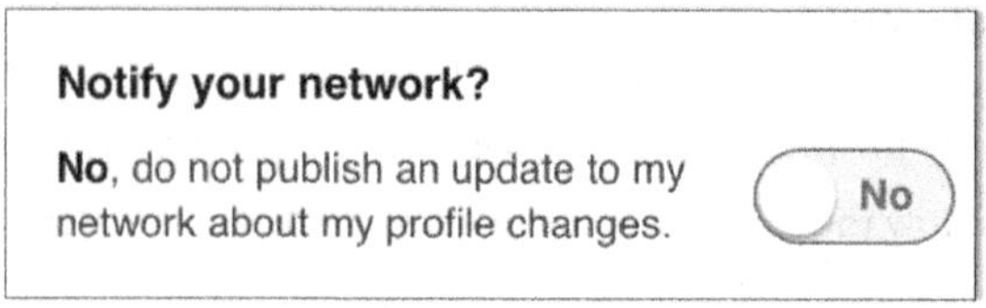

'Ungiven' endorsements

Relationships change. That's life and on Facebook you can defriend the has-beens.

However, because an endorsement is for a specific professional skill, on LinkedIn the endorsements you've given should not be impacted even if relationships change. Nevertheless, it's possible that you mistakenly ticked a request that flashed across your screen. If so, removing it is easy.

1. Go to the Profile of the person you mistakenly endorsed and scroll down to their Skills to where it says Top Skills. Most endorsements are displayed in this section.
2. Choose the skill you've endorsed and move your cursor over the blue plus sign next to it.
3. Hover over the plus sign. It will turn into a minus sign, giving you the option to remove the endorsement.

If the skill is displayed under the ... also knows about section under Top Skills, scroll down to ... also knows about, move your cursor over the blue plus sign as above and remove it when the minus sign appears.

No, a connection is not notified when you remove an endorsement. Yes, you can remove an endorsement even if you're no longer connected to someone.

Endorsements versus recommendations

LinkedIn offers the option to give endorsements.

These 'ticks of approval' should not be confused with recommendations, which must be actively requested and given by someone in the network.

Should you get and give recommendations? Absolutely, as you would in real life. Recommendations are directly linked to a person and particular role (yours and theirs), so are verifiable proof of work and skill.

Next I'll show you how to give, ask for and manage recommendations, including retrospectively.

It takes a bit of effort to get your profile right but once you've done the grunt work, LinkedIn keeps paying off.

MASTERCLASS FOUR: HOW TO USE RECOMMENDATIONS AS SOCIAL PROOF TO ESTABLISH AUTHORITY

So far you've created a profile that packs a punch and have switched off or are managing endorsements to meet industry regulations.

Now add a powerful way to establish credibility and enhance authority: recommendations.

Recommendations link people by company, position and relationship, providing social proof. They position you within a company and industry, allowing others to rank your relative expertise. Displaying relevant recommendations can also help position you for transition into a preferred area by emphasising certain skills over others.

In this Masterclass we look at ways to:

1. Ask for a recommendation
2. Give a recommendation
3. Accept a recommendation or ask for changes
4. Show, hide or move recommendations.

On LinkedIn there are often many ways to do things. To keep it simple, I'll use the way I find easiest. Remember, too, that LinkedIn changes its settings and menus so over time things may vary, but there's a great help section.

With recommendations, the simplest thing to do is go to your Profile and scroll down to Recommendations. You can do most of what you need from there.

Recommendations

Ask to be recommended Manage

Keynote speaker social media leadership & influence
The Social Executive®

Carolyn Hyams
Digital Marketing Director / Passionate about digital marketing at Aquent (incorp. Firebrand Talent & Vitamin T)

“ I've heard Dionne Lew speak at events a number of times and I am always mesmerised by her ability to capture an audience's attention. I recently saw her speak at the Social Media Risk & Reputation Management Forum and prior to that we invited Dionne to speak at our Aquent/Firebrand Talent/Vitamin T Digitalks events both in Sydney and Melbourne. Not only is she... **more** ”

June 24, 2015, Carolyn was with another company when working with Dionne at The Social Executive®

CEO Social Executive® helping boards & executives leverage social media to grow global influence
The Social Executive®

Bronwyn Evans PhD, FIEAust, EngExec, FTSE, CPEng
CEO at Standards Australia

“ I engaged Dionne Kasian-Lew to present to the Standards Australia Board on the impact of emerging digital and social media issues for business strategy and governance. She's a compelling speaker and her incisive thinking and deep understanding of the impact of these mega-trends on business was fascinating. Dionne managed to lay out the global context, economic impacts,... **more** ”

June 13, 2014, Bronwyn was Dionne's client

The difference between recommendations and endorsements

Unlike endorsements, for which LinkedIn offers a too-easy tick or cross prompt, recommendations require effort. While harder to obtain, they are more valuable.

Although not every career path shows steady and logical progression, a leap from retail sales to non-executive director health should prompt questions. When, what, who did they work for? What explains the unusual advancement? Cross-links corroborate claims and the career path that's shown. If someone has falsely claimed to work for a company, people within a network will be able to identify and flag it.

Human resource or reputation managers should do regular audits, but peers can help weed out imposters.

Recommendations also show the relationship between connections; that is, if you managed or reported to someone or if they were a client, teacher or mentor, which helps weight feedback relative to need. If 'team player' is the heart of what you're looking for, recommendations from team members might be a stronger insight than that of the boss. It's all about context.

The absence of recommendations should prompt you to look more closely at a person to ensure that they're legitimate.

Ask for a recommendation

You can reach out to anyone in your network for a recommendation but only approach those you know well and who add value. Unbelievably, I receive requests for recommendations from people I don't know. What they're usually looking for is a product endorsement for something they're selling. LinkedIn is not the right place to do that. Vouching for someone is a big deal.

There are two ways to ask for recommendations:

1. From the Recommendations section on your Profile

2. From Helpful links.

Let's deal with number one.

From the Recommendations section on your Profile

1. Go to Profile and scroll right down until you find Recommendations, usually near the end of the page. Choose Ask to be recommended.

This opens a series of prompts. Follow them.

It's good practice to have a recommendation for each role. You don't have to display them all at once, but you know they're there in case you need them.

2. After selecting a position, choose up to three connections from your network.
3. As you start typing, LinkedIn automatically finds the person you're searching for and requests further details.
4. Fill out the details. When you reach step four a template request is provided.

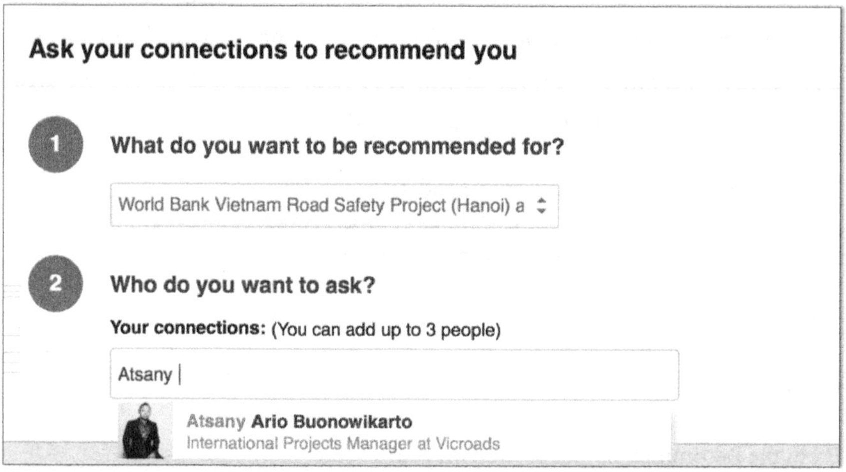

Tailor your message to make it personal and specify the skills you want the recipient to focus on. People are busy. Since you're asking for something, provide prompts that make it easy to action.

Some people ask if it's okay to ask for a recommendation before asking for one (whew – that's a trade-off for manners over email overwhelm if ever I heard one).

If you're polite and willing to accept that your request won't always be granted, you can skip that step.

Write a draft that's not a draft by providing keywords and direction.

For example,

> *"Tom, would you be happy to recommend me for the work I did as stakeholder manager on Project A?*
>
> *I'm applying for a more senior role with the same complex mix of issues and stakeholders on a project with political sensitivities. I think those weekly meetings with the department and Minister's office helped me develop the high-level communications skills they are looking for."*

Push Send. The person will receive an email.

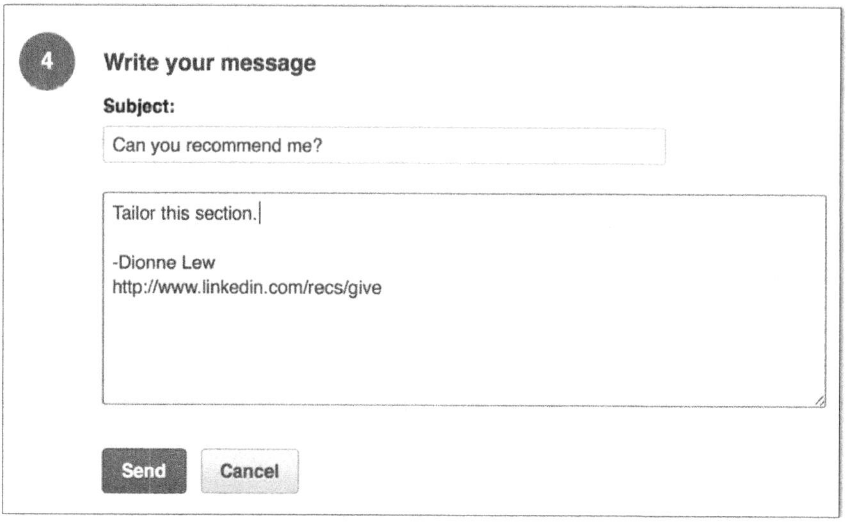

Give a recommendation

Be judicious with recommendations, but give them when warranted.

A recommendation reflects on you so avoid clichés and write well. People need to know you have the qualifications and authority to make a recommendation that matters. Team members send a different message from the boss. They're all important but the context must be clear.

Since time is of the essence, use this simple four-step approach:

1. Open with a bang: Sum up key achievements in a single line.

   "Jane delivered a 50 percent increase in sales over three years by recruiting standout talent and implementing an aggressive training program that created the highest-performance team we've had."

2. Add personal context: Add a line on relative positions and skills, while showing a bit of personality.

   "I had the pleasure of having Jane on my senior executive leadership team. Her strategic and technical advice was second to none and we loved (and miss) her collaborative and witty style."

3. Be specific: Focus on a couple of standout qualities rather many generic ones.

   "I've never seen anyone manage the competing interests of stakeholders with the balance of respect and tenacity to get results that Jane achieved."

4. Hit home: Seal the deal by stating the where and how of their impact.

   "Jane's drive and emotional intelligence will strengthen any leadership team."

There are three ways to give a recommendation:

1. From a connection's Profile
2. From the Recommendations page
3. Responding to a request.

From a connection's Profile

1. Go to a connection's profile, click the arrow next to Send a Message and choose Recommend.
2. Use the template that opens to write a recommendation.
3. Complete the relationship prompts and push Send.

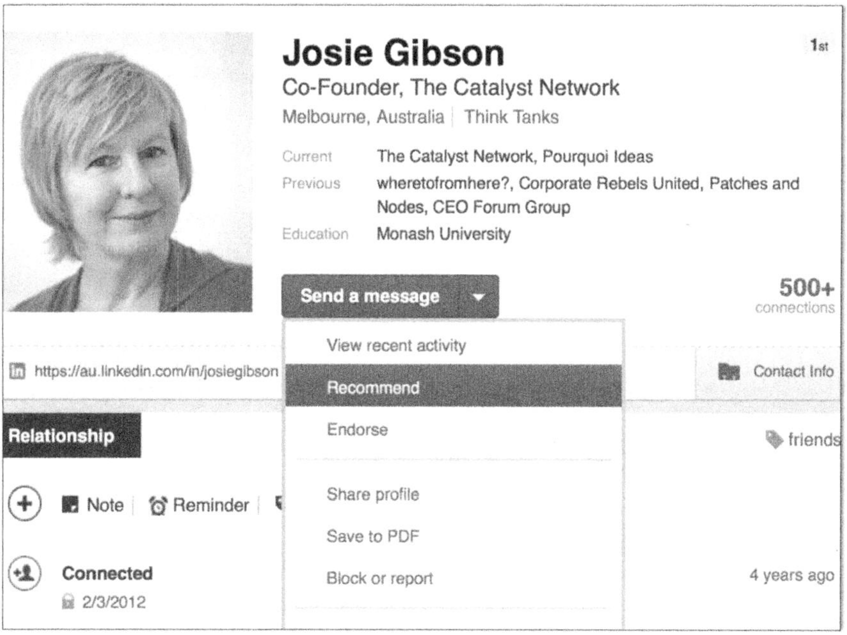

From the Recommendations page

1. From the other person's Profile scroll right down to the Recommendations section.

2. LinkedIn will ask if you want to Recommend the person. If you click the link a series of prompts will open that include the company and role at the time.

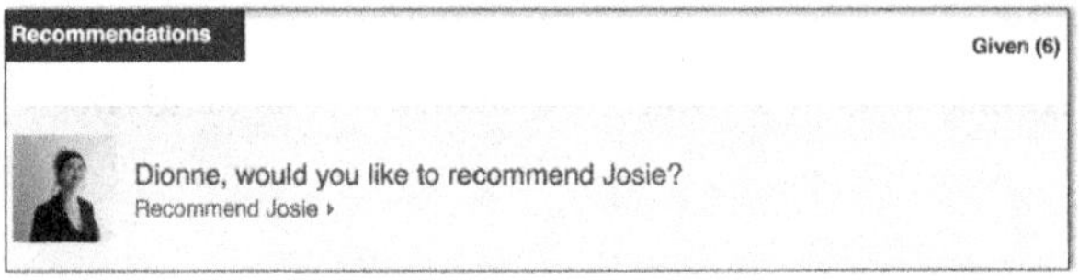

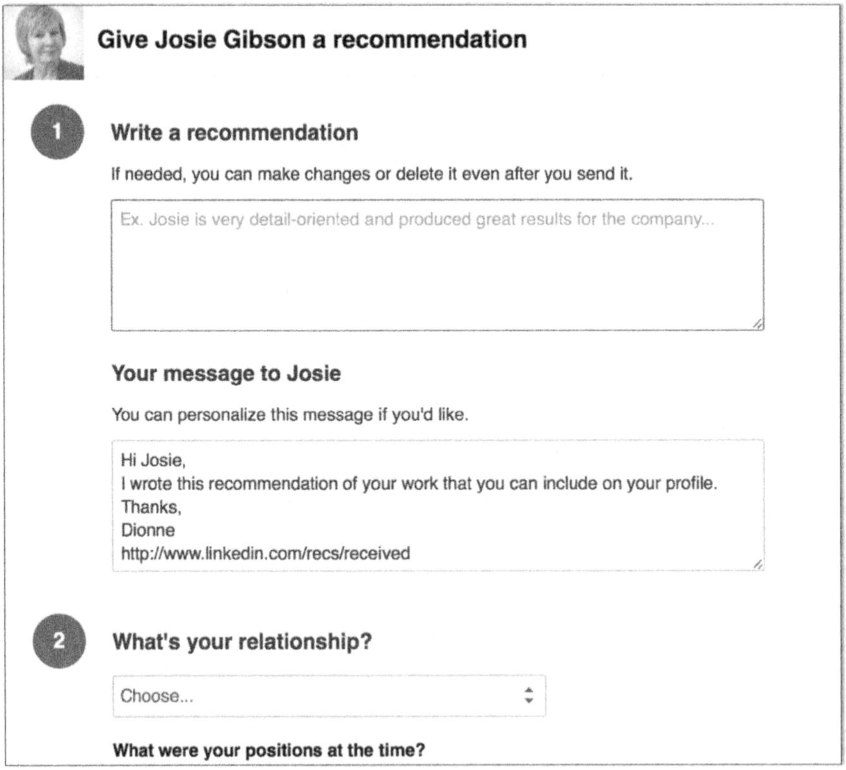

Responding to a request

1. Requests are emailed to the account you've associated with LinkedIn. Open the email and click Write your recommendation, which opens on LinkedIn. I prefer to open recommendation requests on the platform rather than following email links, to avoid phishing scams.

Accepting recommendations

You can accept a recommendation outright or request changes.

From email

1. Open the recommendation in an email titled [Your name], I've recommended you and click Add to profile or Ask for changes first.

From Recommendations

1. Go to your Profile
2. Scroll down to the Recommendations section and click Manage.
3. This opens up a full menu. Go to Received.

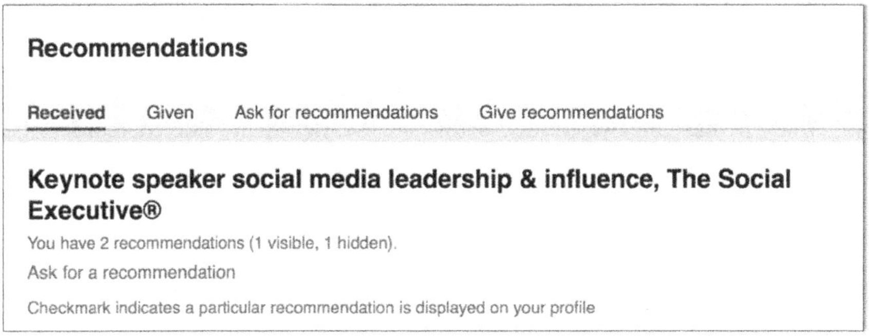

4. Add to profile. You can choose the blue Ask for changes at the bottom of the displayed recommendation.

5. If you don't want the updates sent to your network, remember to turn off the activity broadcast.

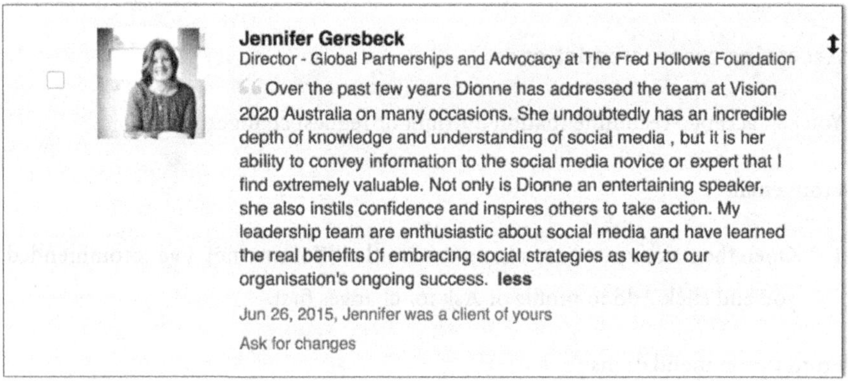

Show and hide recommendations and reorder them

1. Navigate to Recommendations and click Manage.

2. Click on Received. Recommendations will be displayed for each position.

3. Click the box on the left to display a recommendation or leave it empty to keep it hidden.

4. You can use the two-headed arrow on the righthand side to reorder the recommendations you've received by clicking on and dragging them up and down.

Recommendations are the sine qua non of legitimacy on LinkedIn. Used judiciously, they will validate claims and form the bedrock of professional authority.

ABOUT THE AUTHOR

Dionne Lew is a communications executive with 30 years' experience in strategic corporate communications, marketing, media, public relations, stakeholder management, crisis management and online and social media communication.

She is the founding CEO of The Social Executive®, a consultancy advising boards and executives on social media for business, a professional speaker and an author rated top 1% Kred. Her book, *The Social Executive – how to master social media & why it's good for business* (Wiley), is available in bookstores and via Amazon. She is a regular contributor to Forbes, Smart Company, Firebrand Ignition and others.

Dionne was formerly Director of Corporate Affairs at the high-profile government agency, VicRoads, where she led the statewide team for strategic communications, media, web and stakeholder management. VicRoads won more than 40 awards (predominantly in road safety marketing) and was cited by the Victorian Auditor-General in 2012 for effective use of non-traditional media and effective communications strategy.

Dionne is a non-executive director and a graduate of the Australian Institute of Company Directors.

Connect with Dionne on LinkedIn au.linkedin.com/in/dionnelew and Twitter twitter.com/dionnelew and subscribe to TheSocialExecutive.Global to keep learning how social media can help you *Scrub up, stand out and explode your professional brand.*

REFERENCES

Section One

On the importance of social media: http://blog.firebrandtalent.com/2015/05/the-future-of-specialist-social-media-roles/

Boston Consulting Group internet economy report: http://www.bcg.com/documents/file100409.pdf

Capgemini-MIT Sloane: https://www.capgemini.com/resources/the-digital-advantage-how-digital-leaders-outperform-their-peers-in-every-industry

McKinsey: http://www.mckinsey.com/insights/business_technology/cracking_the_digital_code

Social shapes trust

Impact of virtual relationships: http://blog.firebrandtalent.com/2014/06/why-trust-is-the-new-bottom-line-how-social-media-drives-it/

Edelman Trust Barometer: http://www.edelman.com/insights/intellectual-property/2016-edelman-trust-barometer/

Pew on trust from a generational perspective: http://www.pewsocialtrends.org/2014/03/07/millennials-in-adulthood/

Facebook milestone of a billion people active on a single day: http://techcrunch.com/2015/08/27/facebook-hits-1-billion-users-in-a-single-day/

Social influences investors

Investors are influenced by the research they find on social media: http://www.forbes.com/sites/salesforce/2014/09/17/social-media-influences-invest/

FTSE100 Social Media Index: http://library.the-group.net/thegroup/client_upload/file/GRP_Social_Media_update_June_2012%281%29.pdf

Research by Web Profits: http://www.brw.com.au/p/banks_lead_companies_bother_social_FEWvFGAd1TFB06f0RmGF0H

Beaton Research and Consulting for Zurich: http://www.zurich.com.au/content/dam/australia/advisers/Financial-Advisers-and-Social-Media_Zurich-Australia-research.pdf

Survey of Financial Advisors' Use of Social Media: http://www.advisortechtips.com/social-media/financial-advisors-and-social-media/

Social is a part of a multi-trillion-dollar economy

10 percent of GDP in UK: http://www.bcg.com/news/press/1may2015-internet-contributes-10-percent-gdp-uk-economy.aspx

Deloitte's latest report: http://www2.deloitte.com/au/en/pages/media-releases/articles/79billion-australias-digital-economy-grows-and-grows-250315.html

Social impacts markets

Security of Twitter and the quality of control of algorithmic traders: http://www.fastcoexist.com/1681873/twitter-can-predict-the-stock-market-if-youre-reading-the-right-tweets

Whitehaven Coal fake press release: http://www.smh.com.au/business/mining-and-resources/hoax-press-release-sparks-whitehaven-plunge-20130107-2cc47.html

Whitehaven investigated by Australian Securities and Investments Commission (ASIC): https://theconversation.edu.au/public-nuisance-or-fraud-whitehaven-hoax-puts-market-creditability-at-risk-11544

US Securities and Exchange Commission (SEC) allow companies to make corprorate announcements on social media: http://www.sec.gov/News/PressRelease/Detail/PressRelease/1365171513574

ASX-first approach: http://www.businessspectator.com.au/article/2013/4/5/social-media/should-asic-consider-social-media-disclosures

ASX updated guidance on disclosure: http://www.asxgroup.com.au/media/PDFs/guidance-note-8-clean-copy.pdf

Social mentors help shape social leaders

McKinsey Global Survey in 2015: http://www.mckinsey.com/insights/business_technology/bullish_on_digital_mckinsey_global_survey_results

Weber Shandwick: http://www.webershandwick.com/news/article/76-of-global-executives-want-their-ceos-to-be-social

81 percent of executives want a social CEO: http://www.webershandwick.com/news/article/81-percent-of-global-executives-report-external-ceo-engagement-is-a-mandate

Brandfog: http://www.brandfog.com/CEOSocialMediaSurvey/BRANDfog_2012_CEO_Survey.pdf

Statista: http://www.statista.com/statistics/311572/us-uk-employee-opinion-ceo-scocial-media-usage-brand-trust/

Fake followers: http://www.afr.com/technology/why-are-australias-top-ceos-being-swamped-by-twitter-followers--20150903-gje0s8

Issues with executives and other leaders doing a hack job on social: https://meddle.it/content/8a546f544f7a9687014f9900f072612d/public

Why LinkedIn?

Mailguard blog: https://www.mailguard.com.au/blog

Social Selling: https://www.koganpage.com/product/social-selling-9780749478018

Masterclass One: How to scrub up and stand out

Anchor points: http://www.spring.org.uk/2013/05/the-anchoring-effect-how-the-mind-is-biased-by-first-impressions.php

This is not a biography

A title is not a differentiator: https://press.linkedin.com/about-linkedin

Masterclass Two: Amplify your presence – the why and how

Why professionals need an online presence

Best place to hide a dead body is on page two of Google: http://www.huffingtonpost.com/chad-pollitt/the-best-place-to-hide-a-_b_5168714.html?ir=Australia

Over a trillion searches a year on Google: http://searchengineland.com/google-1-trillion-searches-per-year-212940

56 percent of people Google themselves: http://expandedramblings.com/index.php/by-the-numbers-a-gigantic-list-of-google-stats-and-facts/2/

People have a 'right to be forgotten': http://www.wsj.com/articles/hiding-on-the-internet-1440975213

Amplify your presence by integrating Twitter and WeChat

500 million WeChat users: http://www.businessinsider.com.au/wechat-why-it-dominates-china-2015-8

'Quiet giant' of the social web: http://www.smartcompany.com.au/leadership/professional-development/40512-the-benefits-of-using-slideshare.html

Masterclass Three: Enrich and simplify your profile, get 10x more attention

Create a standout LinkedIn profile: http://www.smartcompany.com.au/technology/social-media/49305-linkedin-masterclass-no-1-how-to-scrub-up-and-stand-out.html

Customised, consistent social presence: http://www.smartcompany.com.au/technology/social-media/49604-linkedin-masterclass-no-2-amplify-your-linkedin-presence-the-why-how.html

The brain is wired to respond to visual communication: http://blog.firebrandtalent.com/2016/01/how-to-make-your-content-stand-out-from-the-crowd/

'display, not say': http://blog.hubspot.com/marketing/visual-content-marketing-strategy

Using video for your claims: http://www.convinceandconvert.com/podcasts/episodes/a-volcano-created-a-world-class-social-media-program-for-klm-airlines

Un-endorsing endorsements

Legal consequences for false endorsements: http://www.podlegal.com.au/do-you-really-want-to-be-an-expert/

Industries where accepting endorsements is tricky: http://www.forbes.com/sites/davidmarotta/2014/03/16/five-unbelievable-financial-advisor-regulations/#53717d033e72

Industries where accepting endorsements is tricky: http://www.investmentnews.com/article/20140501/FREE/140509989/linkedin-endorsements-still-a-legal-quagmire-despite-sec-guidance

Industries where accepting endorsements is tricky: http://www.mondaq.com/unitedstates/x/277260/Securities/Finras+Regulation+Of+Its+Members+Use+Of+Social+Media

Industries where accepting endorsements is tricky: http://www.thesocialexecutive.global/investorinfluence/

Industries where accepting endorsements is tricky: http://lifeinthefastlane.com/everyone-really-annoyed-ahpra-social-media-guidance/

Industries where accepting endorsements is tricky: http://blogs.crikey.com.au/croakey/2014/03/27/a-chance-to-get-social-with-ahpra/

Industries where accepting endorsements is tricky: http://www.tresscox.com.au/page/our-news/newsflash/ahpra-updates-the-rules-testimonials-and-social-media-are-in-the-regulators-sights/

Digital and social literacy: http://www.smartcompany.com.au/technology/social-media/42248-are-business-owners-who-don-t-invest-in-social-media-negligent.html

Myths about social media: http://www.smartcompany.com.au/technology/social-media/47393-busting-six-social-media-myths-that-could-be-hurting-your-business.html

Masterclass Four: How to use recommendations as social proof to establish authority

Profile that packs a punch: http://www.smartcompany.com.au/marketing/social-media/49305-linkedin-masterclass-no-1-how-to-scrub-up-and-stand-out/

Manage endorsements: http://www.smartcompany.com.au/technology/62891-linkedin-masterclass-no-3-enrich-and-simplify-a-profile-to-get-40-times-more-attention/

The difference between recommendations and endorsements

Human resource or reputation management audits: http://www.smartcompany.com.au/marketing/social-media/46089-is-lack-of-hr-know-how-in-social-media-negligent/

NOTES

NOTES

NOTES

NOTES

NOTES

NOTES

NOTES

Made in the USA
Monee, IL
04 November 2026

67377193R00046